# CRYSTAL VISIONS

## NINE MEDITATIONS for PERSONAL & PLANETARY PEACE

### by DIANE MARIECHILD
with drawings by Lynn E. Alden

THE CROSSING PRESS
TRUMANSBURG, NEW YORK 14886

Cassette tapes of Diane Mariechild leading some of the meditations in this book are available through The Crossing Press, Box 640, Trumansburg, NY 14886.

**Library of Congress Cataloging in Publication Data**

Mariechild, Diane.
  Crystal Visions

  1. Meditations. 2. Meditation. I. Title.
BL624.M345  1985    131     85-17450
ISBN 0-89594-183-X
ISBN 0-89594-182-1 (pbk.)

## Acknowledgments

With love and thankfulness I honor my brother, Robert, and my sister-in-law, Lea, who cared for me during the first draft of this manuscript. I honor my friend, Kathie, who opened her heart and home to me during a period of most intense transition. Love to Lynn E. Alden who shared her thoughts and feelings about meditation and whose wondrous drawings appear in this book. Thanks to Shuli, whose loving support in listening, reading and editing was invaluable to me; I am happy to know you.

I offer most deep love and respect to the Sunray Community and to my precious teacher, Dhyani. And to Anne, AXOKE.

To my parents,
Marie R. Sherman and M. Frank Sherman,
who gave me the most precious gifts of life and love,
who taught me to express love through service
to family, friends and community.

# Preface

May this book, authored by Diane, inspire its readers to realizing the one truth underlying reality. May all obscurations in individual and planetary mind be transformed that all people may realize their special gifts, and may a most great peace flourish in their hearts and upon the earth. May each reader realize the crystal clarity of mind and know that as each crystal is ever in harmony with the mother crystal heart of the earth, we are all one in the family of life.

The crystal is sacred as an eye of infinity and a representative of the clear light inherent in all beings. In some Native American cultures the crystal is a sacred doorway, a representative of the inherent purity of life. The enclosed crystal meditations are tools for transforming patterns of thought, speech and action that may obscure the pure light within one.

What are obscurations and how will one remove them so that one's inherent potential for good and beauty may be realized? An obscuration is a collection of patterns of thought, speech and action that hinders the manifestation of one's inherent creative potential. Obscurations are fear, doubt, anger, grasping, attraction, repulsion. Fear of success or fear of failure are examples of thought-forms hindering one's bringing forth one's own special gifts. Where do these fears originate? In the Old Native view it is often said that there are only two natural fears: fear of loud noises and fear of falling. All other fears are created within the mind. One way to transform fear is to consider in each moment what "is" rather than what "might be." Generate courage. Where there is repulsion, recognize the field of energy that keeps everything together in the stream. Where there is lust, recognize that there is fulfillment in the moment. Where there is hate, call forth love. There is an antidote for every pattern that obscures the light.

These meditations that Diane has written give one a very simple and basic foundation to begin to transform some of the ideas which we carry about our own nature. This will help bring again the co-creative energy of perception, affirmation and actualization to the front of one's mind.

In this time the form is changing, the cycle is completing and we come to another key in the song of life. Throughout this change, the woman's role is to envision a world of peace and harmony; to clarify within her own consciousness any attitudes of discord. Woman's role is to plant seeds of good relation. By envisioning the heart free of obscurations, she allows conflict to become resolution. Take care, for what we envision and what we speak become reality. The woman's role is a wondrous role. All things are born of the mother. All is born of the emptiness—this is the Great Mystery. Then, through the focus of mind, it becomes female and male, yin and yang. Through this sacred dance the forms are created. All are born of woman and carry that sacred essence in the dance of life. Therefore, the role of all beings is to transmute fear and doubt: to generate generosity and consideration for all beings. So, woman's role is also man's role. It is caretaker role, to take care of one another. Let the mother recall that everyone, whether they have given birth or not, is a parent to our future reality. Let us take responsibility as parents, to create seeds of what is good and beautiful.

The caretaker mind recognizes that we are all relatives; it commits us to bring forth the wisdom in one another. Caretaker mind understands that each individual has a spiritual duty to manifest her or his creative gifts and to find good relationship with family, friends, and co-workers. Caretaker mind knows its special responsibility to the land and to the people of the land, always keeping a prayer that peace may prevail upon the earth. It is the mind that makes peace with one's own heart by putting aside the illusion of "them or us" and recognizing the seed of generosity and good cause.

In these changing times, our minds are bringing forth new visions. Beauty is expressed through the clarification of the heart's inner vision. Peace is affirmed through speech and actualized through harmonious relationship with self and others. As these meditations are done, may the idea of resolution, of transmutation, be realized as peace in your own heart. May the sea of experience resonate out as ripples of grace and peace and may the meditations in this book be good for all beings.

*Dhyani Ywahoo*
*June 1985*

# Foreword

In this time of earth's evolution a critical point has been reached. For Earth to survive, her people must make a choice for peace. Peace comes through the willingness to make peace: individual to individual, family to family, nation to nation. Peace will not be achieved through acts of aggression, conflict or warfare. People of all nations share this in common: earth is our home and we want to survive. The thought-form of conflict, the mind-set of "us and them" must be transformed into a thought-form of unity. Diversity of lifestyles, religious and social rituals and political institutions must become a source of celebration rather than a source of conflict. We must recognize ourselves as a planetary family rather than fighting, nation against nation, to defend territory and resources.

Peace is a personal choice. It begins with the individual willing to make peace with internal conflicts, transforming doubt and fear into certainty and love. Peace grows with the individual's intent to bring peaceful resolution to relationships with family, friends and co-workers. Peace resonates through communities as people turn anger into right action— grow food together, care for elders together, educate children together, elect officials who serve the needs of the people. We must affirm the power of each individual action for peace, however small it may seem.

We must consider in all actions what the effect will be upon the earth and the people for seven generations.

These meditations are a peace offering. Visualizations, affirmation and right action will bring peace on Earth.

*Diane Mariechild*
*July, 1985*

# 1. Three Jewels of Wisdom

This meditation is generously shared by Dhyani Ywahoo. Its purpose is to discover the treasures of the heart. In this meditation we dive deep into the ocean of mind, and from the valleys on the ocean's floor we gather the jewels. These jewels are analagous to the three fires of creation. Each gem exemplifies the energy of one of the fires. The first jewel is the yellow topaz—the light of right action. When we gather this jewel we affirm our willingness to act in harmony with all creation and to work to bring into manifestation what is good for all of life. Swimming to the next valley we gather the ruby—light of compassion. This is the wisdom of forgiving, of releasing pain, shame and blame, that we may see clearly the truth of what is. It is the wisdom of giving, that we may all share in the bounty of the earth. And diving deeper we come to the third gem—the diamond light of clear mind. This is the energy of the will, the light of clear intention. To gather this jewel is to affirm a clarity of mind, to realize ourselves as co-creators of our lives.

## The Meditation

Breathing in and breathing out. Sensing the breath as light. Aware, ever aware of the light. Light spiraling from the heavens, light spiraling from the earth. Aware of yourself as light.

Come, come, come to the ocean's edge. Prepare to enter the sea of light, to swim deeply within the sea of mind, to sense the beauty within. To swim deeply within the mind and gather the jewels from the ocean's floor. Jewels of wisdom, gems of light. Clear sight, that we may see and choose. Compassion, feeling that transmutes and renews. Clear speech/ right action, that we may live in peace.

Enter, enter, enter the cave of your heart. Enter the stream of your knowing. Deep into the waters we go. Three jewels, deep within, treasures gathered in many times. Gems of wisdom in your mind.

Remember, remember, remember, find the way to the treasure within. Swim to the first valley and gather the gem—topaz bright, light of clear speech and right action. Wisdom ever within our life. Gather, gather, gather the gem of light.

Seek, seek, seek ever within the stream of clear knowing. Waters gently washing away thoughts of limitations and fears. Washing clean, thoughts made new. Swimming in the wave. Deep within you the seed of the world unfolds, let us see the way of the Beauty Road.

From the second valley, ruby rose red light. Gather the gem of compassionate wisdom, transmuting ignorance, strife, and fear. Here within your heart. Reach in and bring it forth. Wisdom that renews.

Gathering, gathering, gathering diamond bright, gem of clear sight. In the stream of creation, we share in the dream. Sacred gem of wisdom, let us have clear sight.

See ourselves within a circle of light. Our thoughts are seeds of action. Our words become reality. Speak of peace and love. Come, come, come to the other shore. Free from illusion, realize that our thoughts create. Free from illusion, let us not hesitate. Let us live in peace. Turn the anger into love. Transform the doubt into wisdom. Let us live in peace.*

*From the Tsalagi spiritual tradition passed through Dhyani Ywahoo, Director of the Sunray Meditation Society.

## 2. Child Wisdom

"Child Wisdom" encourages us to remember a time of playfulness and spontaneity, to recall the innate wisdom and purity of our being. One of the ways to remember our life's purpose is to recall those childhood games. What was the most fun for us? What games did we choose again and again? In the game of "let's pretend" we find the seeds of purpose.

We have all suffered from miseducation. Someone knowingly or unknowingly has attempted to stifle our true natures. In this meditation we come again to the peace and joy of the child. The wise person is a joyful child living in harmony with all of creation.

## The Meditation

Sink, sink, sink into the breath. Breathe slowly, breathe deeply. Let the full cycle of the breath remind you of the full cycle of life. Let the complete circle of the breath bring you to the complete circle of life. Let the full circle of the breath become the full circle of life. Giving and receiving. Giving and receiving.

Within you a child is born. Within you a child is given. This is the child of your dreams, born of your knowing. This child is your natural exuberance. This child is your creativity and your delight. This child sings of your playfulness and your joy.

You are here now, present in this moment, no past or future on your mind. You are here now, certain that you are breathing. Certain that you are receiving the gift of the breath, the gift of life. And with this gift you have something to give, something special, something magical to share with us all. This child is the seed of that knowing.

Allow yourself to breathe like that child, baby breath, belly breath, slow and deep. Allow yourself to let go into the moment. Uncover the child within. Uncover the child within.

Sense that child within, feel her moving, dancing, singing. Hear that child's delightful laughter. Sense the freedom as that child moves without fear. Feel the joy of that child emerging. Feel the delight of that child laughing. Know that that child is the peace within. Know that that child is your innate connection with nature, with all that crawls, flies, swims and walks. Know that that child is the goodness, the beauty within. See that child dance and sing.

Come to the source of your knowing. Come to the other shore. Come freely as a naked child, clothed only in the purity of your being. Oh come holy child. You will remember all that is. All that is.

# 3. A Way of Peace

"A Way of Peace" shows us the way of compassion. Through forgiving ourselves and others, through releasing pain, anger and shame, we find peace. Each one of us must honor ourselves as a child of the Earth and we must honor our parents, who are also Earth's children in the process of becoming. Forgiveness is a stream pouring forth from our hearts. In the stream of forgiveness we see all that is. We see the light in everyone, and we see everyone in the process of uncovering that light. Forgiveness does not condone the mistakes of the past. It is the courage to let go of the past and make harmonious relationships in the present. Peace on earth begins with us. Peace is a choice we make.

In this meditation we make peace with our parents, but the meditation can be done with anyone that one is in conflict with. It is a good idea to choose only one or two people at a time. If there are more people to make peace with, do so in separate meditations.

*The Meditation*

The breath, a stream of energy within us, let it flow. The breath, a gift of life, let us give thanks. Breathing in, breathing out. Receiving light, releasing limitations. In and out, in and out. There is no wanting, the circle is filled with space.

Sensing a great stillness, a most great peace. Sensing peace as an understanding of forgiveness, forgiveness and peace as a way of life. Forgiveness, a gift, a stream in which we all swim. Knowing, a gift of understanding through forgiving.

Let a sense of peace stream throughout your entire being. Feel a sense of peace, its fragrance perfuming every cell. Let the sweet scent of peace enfold you and hold you. Focus until you can see the color of peace and feel yourself wrapped within the light of peace, made new again through the light of peace.

Find yourself beside a stream, a river of clean, clear water. Peace flows like this river, when we forgive, letting the hurts of the past give way to the peace of the present. Let the stream wash the pain away. Let the stream wash the blame away. Let the stream wash the shame away. Bathe in the sweet waters of forgiveness. A stream, a stream, a stream of clear light. Clear sight.

Swimming within this river we find peace. Peace, a stream ever-flowing within our hearts. Peace, remembered through forgiveness. Forgiving, releasing, courageously releasing, all the pain of the past. Seeing, clearly seeing veils of shame and blame lifted. Forgiving, letting go, releasing, being one in the moment.

Swimming in this moment is your mother. You are swimming together in this river of love. The water rough around you as the tensions of the past swell. The water swirling with resentments, secrets left unsaid. Your heart blocked through expectations of what could have been or should have been, with pain from feeling deprived, pain from not being understood. Let the water wash away those fears and hurts. Leap through the shame. Leap through the anger. Leap through the pain. Swim now with your mother, a human being in the process of becoming all that she is.

Swimming with you in this moment is your father. Swimming in the river of love. The water rough around you from the resentments of the past. The water swirling with tensions, secrets left unsaid. Heart blocked because of expectations of what could have been or should have been. Pain from not getting enough, from not being recognized as you are. Pain and blame from the past washed away in the river. Leaping through the anger, leaping through the blame. Swimming with your father, a human being in the process of becoming all that he is.

Know the peace that comes through forgiveness. Know the peace that is. Swim with yourself, a human being in process of becoming all that she is. Know the love that flows from your heart as you honor yourself as whole. Know the peace that comes from your heart as you honor your parents as whole. Receive the gift of your family. Understand that which you have been given. Receive the gift of life.

Realize yourself, a whole/holy being. Swim to the other shore, the shore of your knowing. Stand free in the knowledge that you are love. Love is your birthright. Awaken to the love that is you. Awaken to the nature of you. Awaken to the compassion that is you. Awaken to the peace that is you.

## 4. Crystal Visions

"Crystal Visions" is a means for remembering our special purpose and gifts. In the crystal cave we have an opportunity to observe, without clinging to either the good or the bad, the experiences of our lives. In this way we come to see the patterns as they unfold. This helps to make our choices clear. Within the crystal cave we have the opportunity to transmute whatever calls for transmutation. The violet light of the rainbow has the highest vibratory rate of all colors. This high rate of vibration enables transmutation to occur. Then, when the mind is clear of hindrances and limitations, the purpose of this life may be recalled. One may observe in this crystal cave the gifts and understandings that are unique to each and may see the means to fully develop them for the good of all life.

*The Meditation*

Breathe, breathe, breathe, deep into the center of yourself.
Feel your body light and free. Come, come, come deep within
the center of the earth. Feel your body light and free. Whirling, swirling deep within the center of the earth. Singing,
singing, your heart singing, light of compassion pouring
forth. Whirling, swirling deep within the center of the earth.

Gently you land within an empty cave, deep in the heart of
the earth. And in the center of the cave, suspended from the
ceiling, a huge crystal rotates slowly, casting rainbow lights
across the rocky room. As the crystal rotates, irradiating the
room with light, you see in its reflections the string of all of
your lives. In this moment is the opportunity to realize all
that you have carried with you. In this moment is the opportunity to realize your choice. See clearly your path, the
lessons of your lifetimes, the gifts of your mind unfolding
gently before your eyes.

Crystal spinning slowly, casting light across the room. See
the wisdom unfolding within you. With crystal clarity, mind
ever bright, see what calls for transformation. See what calls
to transmute. Crystal clear, crystal bright, recognizing how
to build anew from the constituents of the past.

Mind clear, heart open as the crystal spins around. Crystal
light, wisdom dance, all seen within a glance. Past, present,
future swirl around you now. In this sacred space, the crystal
visions of your heart sing out. Let the purpose be known. Let
the purpose be known. Crystal vision, crystal dream. Beauty
of what is. Life of love, life of light, tapestry woven bright.
Sense the sacred circle, a holy web of light. Hear the crystal
singing, it sings out a crystal song. See the means, see the
way, unfolding in your heart.

Return from the crystal cave, heart singing its purpose.
Awaken your crystal beauty. Let it shine.

## 5. Compassionate Being

"Compassionate Being" is a meditation of purification and forgiveness. It is a means for opening the heart and receiving and giving compassion. We visualize a Holy Mother who feeds and cares for us. Through her nurturing and sustenance we are able to release limitations of mind and realize the completeness of each moment. We make an offering of our suffering, and it is transformed into food to feed all people. We recognize that this Holy Mother is us. Within our hearts is the compassionate energy of life that nourishes all the people. When suffering is released, the energy of love flows freely. Good cause is created when we meditate in this way and this is not for ourselves alone. We share the good cause with all beings. In this way we are working for both personal and planetary transformation.

*The Meditation*

Breathe deeply, inhaling the energy of the earth. Exhale completely, sending the energy of the earth into the sky. Breathe in, drawing the energy of the sky into your being. Breathe out, sending that energy deep into the heart of the earth. Breathing in and out, receiving the energy of earth and sky, sensing yourself, comfortably seated within this double vortex of energy and light.

Now see before you a calm, clear lake. Arising from the lake is a most beauteous lotus blossom and, seated on that lotus blossom, a most compassionate being, a Holy Mother of all, giver of love, laughter and life. Her eyes are clear and bright. There are no barriers here, only space. She is dressed in silk, with flowers in her hair, and in her hands is a brilliant crystal, a wish-fulfilling gem. A calm, sure strength radiates from her being. Her smile is confident and tender. Total acceptance, pure love, is the essence of her being, and the light of compassion swirls from her heart and fills the surrounding space. From her breasts flows a sweet nectar and, as this nectar flows, it washes over you, purifying you, feeding and sustaining you. As the sweet nectar washes through you, all doubt and pain is washed away and you are filled with a deep sense of peace and contentment. Sweet nectar washing over you, you are fed, you are at peace.

As the nectar continues to flow over and through you, imagine that all your fears, any limitations of mind, are leaving your body in the form of a dark, smokey liquid that pours from you into the earth. The sweet nectar of the Holy Mother's love flows through you, cleansing you of all pain and suffering. And all your fears, like smokey liquid, pour into the earth.

As the smokey liquid leaves your body and flows into the earth, it is transformed into sweet nectar. The earth opens up and in the center of the earth are all those people who are wanting something from you. All the people with whom your relationship is not yet clear are calling out from the center of the earth. All those people you feel you need to ask for forgiveness and all those you need to forgive are there in the center of the earth. And the smokey liquid leaving your body, is transformed into nectar which feeds these people. They, too, are satisfied and no longer wanting. Let the liquid from your body, transformed into nectar, feed these people so that they are filled with a deep sense of peace.

Breathing in and out as the sweet nectar fills you, you are clear as a crystal. As you breathe in and out, knowing your crystal clarity, the vision of the Holy Mother dissolves into light and, as you inhale, you inhale that light. You are infused with that light. Sense the wonder of the Holy Mother, giver of life, love and laughter, within you. Know that you, too, are a most compassionate being, heart as open as the sky, filled with space and wanting nothing. Know that this is the truth of your being. Breathing in and breathing out, sending waves of loving kindness from your heart to the hearts of all people, to the heart of the earth. And breathing in, receiving waves of love from the hearts of all people, from the heart of the earth. Know that you are love and love radiates from the very heart of your being. Awaken with this energy of love flowing from you and to you.

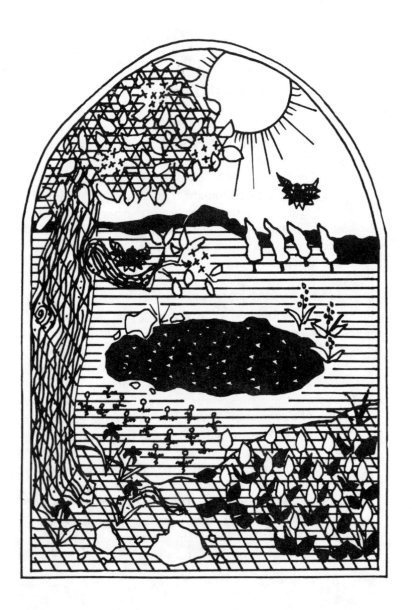

## 6. Earth Dance

In "Earth Dance" we acknowledge ourselves as children of the Earth, connected to and sustained by the Earth, our mother, who gives us all that we need. Native Americans were taught that Earth is a living being, a gracious mother, who feeds the hearts and bellies of all people. They were told that everything they needed was here within and upon this global paradise, that, if needed, corn would grow out of a rock. The earth's resources will again become abundant through our sharing and practicing generosity. Generosity of thought is holding only thoughts of harmony, of abundance, of love and peace for all. Generosity of words is speaking the best of yourself and everyone. Generosity of action is forgiving and giving, creating what is good for all. To think of ourselves as consumers of the earth's resources is to abuse the earth; to think of a continuous cycle of reciprocity, of giving to the earth and receiving from it, aids in creating abundance.

In this meditation we attune to the energy of the elements and receive their teachings. We visualize the rainbow connecting heaven and earth so that we may transform any energy that is calling for transformation. In this way we enable the abundant energy of the earth to dance through us and all beings.

## The Meditation

Feel yourself relaxing now, quickly and easily, one with the flow of your breath. Your breath is slowing and deepening and your body begins to slow with your breath. Slowly moving, moving into the stillness, into the silence within. Turning inward, turning inward, a slow and spiraling dance.

Feel the quiet in your body as your muscles relax and release any tension. Feel the quiet in your mind as your thoughts become still. Let the velvety blackness, the richness of the dark, surround you and enfold you as you move more deeply into that dark rich void. Moving into the void, moving into the emptiness, moving into the formlessness through which all form is birthed.

And in the darkness hearing a sound, the song of the Holy Mother. And as she sings her name, the sound becomes light and form, the sound shapes patterns, dancing, forming all worlds.

Traveling inward on a beam of light, moving with softness, moving with grace, to the place where the Earth calls you. Sense the movement, sense the pulse, sense the dance of the Earth. Hear the Earth sing out, calling you to a place of wonder, a place of power.

Find yourself in this paradise now. Visualize yourself making an offering of the smoke of cedar and sage to the four directions and to heaven and earth. Pray for all your relations. Honor the guardians of the North—the wisdom of the mirror lake, the wisdom that reflects. Let the smoke carry your prayer to the East—the gift of the eagle's sight, the power of dream and intuition. Honor the guardians of the South—the wisdom of renewal, the generosity of the Corn Mothers. Let the smoke carry your prayer to the West—the wisdom of recycling, the bear's dance, the gift of transformation.

Sit with the beauty of the land. Know that each of the elements within the earth is within your body. Know that the elements are teachers, medicine helpers. Let the elements speak through you.

Listen, listen, listen to the sound of the wind dancing through you. Listen to the song of the wind. Singing, sighing, whispering wind. Element of air, energy of thought. Listen to the song of the wind.

Listen, listen, listen to the sound of the water. Let its message resound. Watch the dance of the water, swirling, pulsing water. Gentle stream, gentle waves, wash against the shore. Element of water, energy of emotion. Listen to the song of the water.

Hearing, sensing, seeing, feeling. Warmth of the sunlight on your skin. Dance of the sunlight on the water, patterns of light through the leaves. Element of fire, energy of transformation. Fire, fire, warming and opening the door to your heart.

Sense the pulse of the Earth. Feel the dance of the Earth. Listen to the heart of the Earth. Know that if there is suffering it can be transformed. Call upon the energy of the Earth and the heavens, bridged by the rainbow. The violet light of the rainbow is the energy of transformation. May your unmanifested potential be realized through the transformation of any hindrances. May the energy of conflict be transformed by the violet light into the energy of peace. May our hearts and the heart of the Earth beat as one.

Sing the song of the Crystal Mother of the Earth. Awaken to the dance of the Earth. Awaken to a world of peace.

## 7. Rainbow Warrior

"Rainbow Warrior" affirms our commitment to be spiritual warriors, beings of light dedicated to maintaining peace through harmonious relationships with all of life. The warrior is at war with ignorance, that which hinders one from knowing the true reality — that we are all in relationship, all of one family. The sword of the warrior cuts through the hindrances. The warrior maintains peace of heart through the courageous choice to throw doubt and fear into the fire of transformation and to ever wash in the waters of regeneration, the waters of forgiveness. The warrior transforms doubt into wisdom, sorrow into joy, dishonesty into truth, jealousy into caring, and anger into right action.

*The Meditation*

Spirals of light, pillar of light. Seated within the light. Breathing in, breathing out, certain of the light.

Within you resides a warrior, a warrior of the light, a warrior of the rainbow. She is a powerful woman, she is a woman of power. She expresses her power in unique and wonderful ways. She is a wise woman. She is a woman who is wise. She is a strong woman. She is a woman who is strong. She is an intuitive woman. She is a woman who is intuitive. She is a woman who is prepared to meet the challenges of this time. She is a woman of strong, clear will. She is a woman of clear intention. She is a mindful woman. She is a woman, awake. Within you is a warrior, a woman of light.

The warrior is a woman of peace. She is able to turn aside anger, transforming it into compassionate action. The warrior is a woman whose heart is filled with compassion. She sees the suffering and encompasses it. The warrior is a woman of clear action. She can act with lightning speed. She can act with great circumspection. The warrior realizes the unity of all life. The warrior walks within the sacred circle of life. The warrior walks the path of balance. The warrior is a woman walking. The warrior is a peaceful woman walking. She is walking the path of the rainbow, the path to our deepest wisdom, the wisdom of the heart.

Hear the beat of your heart. Hear the beat of a drum. Let the drumbeat of your heart carry to the warrior. You are traveling on a road of light, traveling on a road to the sea. Traveling on a rainbow road. Here along the rainbow path you will meet the rainbow warrior, the clear thinking, clear acting, compassionate being who wields a sword of light. You will know her well. She is a being who has made a commitment to the light by serving the light within herself and within all beings.

You see the warrior now. And you walk with this warrior-woman until you come to the place of the sacred fire. Here the fire of transmutation is built. You dig the pit. Place the

stones, lay the sticks. Light the fire. Let the smoke be an offering that the flame, the light, be clear within you. As you
hear the crackling sound of the fire and watch the smoke
curling in the air you can cast into that fire any doubt or fear.
This is the fire of transformation. Here you can drop the
shroud of your pain. Here you have the opportunity to drop
any patterns or habits that have obstructed the clear light of
mind. You make the courageous choice to let go of the pain
and hurt of the past. And as you release your pain you realize
that this fire of transformation always burns within you.
Within your center burns a sacred fire in which you can
dispel any thoughts of separation or scarcity.

Now the fire has burned down. You and the warrior
woman leave together. You leave the ashes and walk to the
edge of the stream. In this stream you wash away any remain-
ing guilt or pain. The water, a stream of forgiveness, washes
over you. As it streams down your back, as you bathe in the
water, you forgive yourself. You wash away that which needs
to be washed away. Forgive yourself for not meeting needs
and expectations of self and others. Forgive yourself for errors
of the past, for that which was left undone. In this moment
be washed free.

And if there is one that you were not able to treat with
kindness and care, forgive yourself for that. If there is one
that did not treat you with respect and care, forgive them.
Have the courage to let this experience be washed from you
so that you no longer resonate with the energy of pain,
shame or blame. Bathe in the waters of forgiveness. Know
that through forgiving yourself you can forgive others. See in
that stream family and friends in right relationship. Know
that forgiveness is a most courageous choice. To forgive is to
give. To forgive is to be present in the moment, free of guilt
and fear. To forgive is to come to the clarity of ourselves, to
remember the rainbow way. To forgive is not to condone
mistakes of the past; it is to make right in the present. To
forgive is to release suffering so that we can move in clarity
and joy. Dive deep in the water. Be washed clear.

With mind clear and heart opened, you realize that you are the warrior woman. And you stand upon the path, a most courageous warrior. See yourself moving from the space of the warrior, with no past or future on your mind. See yourself fully present, awake in the moment. You are a warrior, a world server, dedicated to the manifestation of peace on earth, through the radiance of peace of heart and the deep commitment to peaceful resolution in all your relationships.

Awaken with the heart and mind of the warrior. Awaken to a world of peace.

## 8. Temple of the Sisterhood

"Temple of the Sisterhood" recognizes teachers of light, beings in other dimensions who serve us, who are dedicated to the manifestation of truth and harmony throughout all creation. These beings live in the angelic realm. Some call this the devic realm, others the pure land, and others the crystal realm. What is important is to realize that we are not alone, that we have guidance and help as we travel through this life. We receive this guidance when we are willing to quiet the mind and open to it. In this meditation we have an opportunity to again affirm our life purpose and to look into the future and plant seeds of harmony for our next life.

*The Meditation*

Inhaling and exhaling. Inhaling and exhaling. Breathing in the earth and exhaling it into the sky. Breathing in the sky and exhaling it into the earth. Inhaling and exhaling.

Sensing the meeting of heaven and earth within your heart. Sensing the double helix of light within your body.

Wrapped in a shimmering cloak of light you spiral inward through clear, pale, aquamarine light. Spiraling inward through a vortex of light. Dazzling light, brilliant streams of light, swirling over and through you. Singing colors of light, irridescent beams of light spiral you deeper and deeper until you gently come to rest on the top of a mountain.

Here in the stillness of the mountain top, through the purple mist, you see a small temple and you see, moving from the temple, moving through the mist, hooded, robed figures, floating silently by. You have entered the Temple of the Sisterhood. You have walked through the mist, walked through the dream. Here abide these gracious beings of light, teachers who are witness to your passage through this life and the next. They are here to serve you, to honor you, to guide you. These most compassionate and wise beings live a life of joyful and devoted service that you may realize all that you are.

The figures silently beckon to you to enter their dance, their circle of light. As you move together the dance begins. There are seven circles, seven rings of luminous light. Brilliant spirals of light, dancing patterns of light, you receive guidance from these most holy beings. Sensing the most wonderous gift of pure mind, you recognize your purpose, see those special gifts that are yours to refine and share.

Seven circles of light, seven rings of light. Dancing, dancing, you receive the guidance of these beings, sensing clearly your next life, sensing clearly how to manifest more fully the beauty that you are.

Whirling, swirling patterns of light, slowly spiraling lights. Dancing, ever more slowly until once again the circle is still. The sisters silently drift into the mist and you are standing alone. Then wrapped in your cloak of light you spiral through the aquamarine light, returning to the present.

## 9. The Medicine Wheel

"The Medicine Wheel" is a meditation to manifest world peace. Through the honoring of the peoples of all directions, through the visualizing of all these people living in harmony, we can bring a most great peace to this world. To the Native Americans the Medicine Wheel is a mandala, a mirror of mind, the whole universe. And everything that walks, crawls, swims and flies is contained within the wheel. Every tree, rock, and river is within that wheel. And all these things have their place. And all these things live in harmony. We must learn to open our hearts, to touch, to sense our relationship with all of life. And we must choose now to build right relationships, to walk in balance with all of life.

*The Meditation*

Breath of heaven, breath of earth, meeting in your heart. Breathing in and breathing out, light within your heart.

Mirrored within your heart, a medicine wheel, the wheel of the universe, container of all things. Breathe in the medicine wheel. Breathe out the medicine wheel. Honor the sacred circle of life.

Breathing in and breathing out, simply, very simply. The medicine wheel is the circle of life, a mandala of mind, the journey we make through this world. Each of us comes from a particular direction and we all meet in the center. The medicine wheel, circle of life. Everything that walks, crawls, flies, and swims is within this circle. And everything within this circle, within this medicine wheel, is our relative. We have a relationship with everything within this circle. And it is our prayer that our relationship is right, that our relationship is whole, that our relationship is balanced.

Breathing in and breathing out, simply, very simply. Let us honor the four directions. Let us turn and face the four directions.

In the North, resting place of the thunderbird, home of the buffalo, we learn wisdom through repeated action. Here frozen in the mirror lake are the thoughts that have created cause in our lives.

And as the ice begins to thaw and the stream again flows we come to the East where the eagle flies to the sun. In the East we recognize ourselves as individuals, within a strong community of beings. In the East we sense good relationships within our communities.

In the South are the seeds of our potential. In the South we gather the seeds of potential, the seeds of renewal. We honor the Corn Mothers, those gracious beings who plant seeds of good cause through the practice of generosity.

And from the South, carrying tradition, the Grandmother, on our backs, we cross over to the gate of the West. Here in the West is the opportunity to recycle, to transform, to throw into the fire all our doubt and fear.

Hear we dance with the great bear, dance upon the pyre of our illusions and come again to the North where we recognize our will aligned with the great will, the divine will.

Breathing in and breathing out, let us dance around the medicine wheel. Let us dance the dance of peace. Let us see the children of every direction, loved and cared for. Let us see the elders of every direction, respected and cared for. Let us see all people living in right relationship with each other and the earth. Let us visualize a world of enlightened action, a world of beauty, a world of peace.

Breathing in and breathing out. Knowing that we are all pregnant with the world to come. Knowing that peace is a seed, a child within us. And we can nurture that child by nurturing each other. Breathing in and breathing out, let us dance the dance of peace. Let us sing the song of peace. In our hearts and in our minds, through all our actions, let the sacred hoop be renewed.

## Concepts and Practice

I saw a great circle, a wheel of light, turning, turning, turning. And as the wheel turned I realized that each of us is a spoke in that great wheel of light. And it is necessary for each individual spoke to be strong for that wheel to turn. Each of us is both an individual, a spoke, and a part of a whole, the wheel. We follow our individual paths while emerging from and returning to the same source or center.

A living vision is a mystery to be explored. It is too vast to be contained in words, yet the words are keys for further exploration. Through continued contemplation of this wheel of light, its truths gently unfold. This vision is my friend, my teacher, and as I continue to explore my relationship to this vision I deepen my understanding of the circle of life. The vision has shown me again and again that we are all whole in ourselves and part of a sacred circle, the circle of light. Our true nature, our essence, is this light, and we can all trace our roots to this same source of light. Within this circle each individual is necessary and has a sacred duty to refine and strengthen their innate gifts for these gifts are needed to make the wheel turn, needed for the survival, the good of all of life. Everything is contained within this sacred circle and respect for the sacredness of all keeps this wheel bright, keeps this wheel turning. As I reflect on this image of the wheel I deepen my understanding of my individual purpose and how that is part of a whole dream, the dream of a world of enlightened beings sharing together and living in a way that is balanced and peaceful.

The wheel of light was shown to me a number of years ago when I began my studies with Dhyani Ywahoo of the Ani Gadoah Clan of the Tsalagi (Cherokee) Nation. The Native American teachings are very dear to my heart. Here is a tradition where the knowledge that we women have in our very bones is respected. The Great Mystery is an empty womb from which all things are brought forth. All matter is mother. "From the emptiness came a sound," say the ancient ones, and this sound, this vibration, gave birth to all that is. All of life is sacred and this sacredness, this wholeness, is a seed within all. The mother is honored; nothing is born without the mother. It is the caretaking energy of the mother that nourishes what is good for all of life. And all of us are mothers—whether or not we give birth to children, we give birth to our thoughts. And we must take care with our thoughts, for "as we see, so shall it be." In the Native American tradition all life exists within a circle, where all are equally respected and necessary. There is no greater than or lesser than within the circle; we are all relatives.

Relationship is a most precious gift and we honor the relationship of self to self, self to process, self to other, self to planet and self to universe. In the relationship of self to self one recognizes that one is worthy to be alive; self-doubt is dissolved. One energetically works to discover and bring forth their individual gifts as a service for all of life. In the relationship of self to the process of unfolding, one recognizes self as unique and part of a planetary family. With loving kindness, one recognizes mistakes, forgives self and affirms right action. In the relationship of self to other, one recognizes that seed of most pure light within each person and makes clear in one's heart the commitment to complementary resolution, to seeing all as equals in a process of unfolding, and one forgives and gives. One chooses to affirm what is good/whole in oneself and others. In the relationship of self to planet one recognizes that self and planet are in bio-resonant relationship, that the individual's actions and thoughts have a direct relationship to the elements of the earth. One recognizes oneself as a caretaker of the earth and through honoring the natural flow of reciprocity, one respects and keeps abundant the earth's resources. In the relationship of self to universe one recognizes the infusion of the spirit throughout the cosmos and seeks to align oneself in harmony with the energy of creation which exists within each individual as a spark waiting to be rekindled.

This spark can be rekindled through meditation. The practice of meditation is a very ancient one, hundreds of thousands of years old. It is a gift, a means for observing the nature of one's mind and its relationship to the cosmos in any given moment. There are both active and receptive spaces in the process of meditation. We are active when we choose to meditate, when we chant or hold a certain visual image, and we are receptive when we sit with the breath, aware of the light moving through us. We become active again when working to actualize the perceptions received in meditation. In this process the active and receptive parts may change according to the moment; one may observe until the observed and the observer become one. Through the practice of meditation, through the careful observation of the stream of thoughts, we come to a space where the thoughts are stilled, we come to the spaciousness of our being. Our true nature is as empty as the sky, filled with space, wanting nothing. In this spaciousness we realize that we are the sky, our thoughts the clouds arising and dissolving.

The Native American concept of emptiness is similar to that of the Buddhists. We come from emptiness and carry within us this emptiness. Our true nature is emptiness. What we see as self arises from that emptiness. In reality there is no self. What we often think of as the self is actually a group of concepts, forms, feelings, perceptions, and consciousness. The self as self doesn't exist. It is simply a description of the dynamics of these five groups. A way to look at this might be by asking oneself the question "What is a car?" Is it the frame?

Is it the motor? Is it the wheels? The car doesn't actually exist, yet when we put these things together we have what is known as a car. Another way to explore this concept is to ask, "Who am I?" If I identify with my job and I lose it, who am I? If I identify with a certain person and we separate, who am I? If I identify with walking and I can no longer walk, who am I?

Everything in the universe is in a continual state of change and flux. When our body changes, or when our thoughts or perceptions or feelings change, then who are we? What is our essential nature?

Our true nature is very peaceful. When we no longer cling to a particular thought, concept, person, place or thing we begin to experience a sense of spaciousness. The breath is the gift of life. Through the observation of the breath we come to know what we can be sure of: that we are breathing. The breath is coming in and going out—a continuous cycle, ebbing and flowing. Constant motion, constant change. Do we have the courage to awaken to the present, to be fully here, at peace, without clinging, certain in the motion of change?

Through the practice of meditation we have the opportunity to uncover our true nature. This uncovering is a process of gradual unfolding that calls for courage, discipline and perseverance. In this hectic world we have forgotten to make time for meditation, for daily contemplation. We are so busy *doing* that we have forgotten how to *be*. We must be willing to make the time for meditation and to recognize that meditation is as important as our other daily activities. We may fear that meditation is an escape, a waste of time. In the pain born of the mind that separates, we may think that we must choose either to be an activist working for world peace or a meditator seeking peace within herself. We think we must choose between the material world or the spiritual world. In reality there is no separation. All things are infused with the spirit. There can be no world peace without individuals finding peace of heart and mind and peace within their family, friend and work relationships. To be a whole person is the challenge of today. To bring the awakened mind to each task, however large or small, is what is being asked of us today.

Meditation is a pathway home. Through sitting and observing the stream of mind, one learns non-reaction. This is the ability to remain centered and without attachment to the patterns and thoughts that arise. To recognize, "oh, a thought arising, I am not that thought," enables one to make a clear choice. This I will do, this I will not do. We can choose to amplify those thoughts and actions that affirm our wholeness and to release those that do not. Our true nature is pure and clear as a crystal. We are majestic beings, holy goddesses, warriors, queens.

We often mistake the habits and reactions learned in years of miseducation and misunderstanding for our essential selves. We have been taught to doubt ourselves, to feel that we are not good enough, not deserving, and these feelings of scarcity give rise to anger, pain and blame, and cause much suffering. We have been taught to argue, compete, defend, debate, to think that we are better than or less than others. These incorrect attitudes of mind come from a false sense of pride, from an arrogance that causes us to feel separate. Whenever we feel we are better than or less than another we feel separate and we need to reaffirm that we are all within a circle of life. We have all had painful experiences and, even though we may no longer be in the situation that caused us pain, we carry that pain in our mind and in our energy fields, often perceiving present situations through the lens of that pain. The mind tends to grasp, to cling, so we hang onto these painful experiences and build up a hardness around our hearts. The mind tends to identify with the feeling; we think, "I am angry," rather than, "I have a feeling of anger." As these feelings, and habits of thought and action accumulate the true nature of the self becomes forgotten, covered over.

Through the practice of meditation we gradually peel away

layer after layer, and, as in peeling away the layers of an onion, the peeling process often causes tears. Yet, when it is complete, nothing of the old self is left. What is revealed is nothing, no-self, the emptiness. This is the vast sea that contains all possibilities. This is the sky, spacious, limitless. We are free.

We are, by nature, courageous. The only natural fears a baby is born with are the fear of loud noises and the fear of falling. All other fears are created by the mind and can be released through mindfulness, through becoming fully aware. We must call upon our courage and come face to face with the learned limitations and fears the mind has created. The mind's tendency to cling creates a certain discomfort when we are working to release fears. The closer we come to our true nature, the more the mind tends to grasp at the old definitions of self. We can feel like we are getting worse rather than better. Whatever has been obscuring the light of the natural self is brought to the surface. The fire, the heat that is generated through the increasing clarity of mind causes the deeper hindrances to boil and bubble up to the surface. Do we have doubts about our ability, strength or goodness? Does our false pride say that we are better than or less than someone else? Do our judgments increase in number and intensity? Do we feel that we don't have enough time or resources or love? Does our greed make us grasp for the most blissful experience? Does our laziness blame someone or something for preventing our freedom? Do we become overwhelmed by intense anger or shame? We need strenuous discipline and courage to stay with this process of mindfulness and not grasp at and identify with the content of our mind. This means that we become a witness. We observe the stream of thoughts without being attracted or repelled by them. We see the thoughts as energy moving and allow it to move without suppressing or expressing it.

Ideally, one looks towards developing a time for daily meditation and contemplation. Fifteen minutes to an hour is a good length of time. It may be helpful to begin with shorter meditation times and gradually increase them. Growth is cyclical so there will be times when it will be very easy to meditate and one will have plenty of time. Other times meditation will be last on the list of activities. Sometimes the energy will flow easily and other times it will be most uncomfortable as the hindrances of mind come to the surface. It is important to make the intention clear, "I will meditate," and to have perseverance, patience and kindness towards self in the process.

Through the practice of meditation we come to a new and deeper understanding of ourselves and the world around us. The mind becomes clearer and the life energy stronger. Eventually the clarity of mind that is experienced during the meditation becomes the daily consciousness.

An excellent time for meditation is in the morning before starting one's daily activities. This sets the tone for the day. We have a clearer and stronger energy when we begin with a prayer of thankfulness for this life and the opportunity to grow, to share and to know. In the practice of meditation we come to a calm and centered place. We can move about our lives from this center and not be so easily pushed to and fro by the events around us. Meditation gives us an opportunity to practice balance and equanimity, to clearly choose those things we will act upon and those things we will not. It releases us from reactive mind, in which we respond to situations, emotions, and people outside ourselves.

Other excellent times for meditation are sundown or the time before sleep. At these times we have the opportunity to be thankful for the day, to look at what was a complete action and to affirm it and to look at what is incomplete and affirm that it will be complete when the opportunity again arises. We can let go of any disturbing experiences so that they will not accumulate in our bodies or energy fields. Then, relaxed and centered, we are open to receiving the blessings of the dream.

Why are we always giving thanks for our many opportunities when often we have painful and disturbing experiences or feel that our opportunities are so limited? We are looking to develop an attitude that sees no blame, pain or shame. This attitude allows us to recognize the power of the individual as co-creator of the world. As co-creator we see that there are no absolute "rights" or "wrongs." There are only choices to make, and actions and reactions that spring from these choices. Through our practice we learn to make clearer choices that are good for ourselves, those around us, and the earth. Our practice reaffirms our deep connection with all of life—that we live on the same planet, that we breathe the same air, that the same sun shines upon us all, that we are part of the same field of energy, that each individual journey is important for the whole circle. Each individual coming to greater clarity makes a path for others to do the same. And that clear energy feeds our Mother Earth, for the same elements that constitute the earth constitute our bodies. So giving thanks is a way of returning to the Earth some of the bounty she has given us. This keeps the cycle of reciprocity flowing and is a way of transforming the mind-set of "I don't have enough" or "Why did this happen to me?" to one of self-empowerment: "I can choose to respond to this," and "I can look to see the teaching in this moment, however painful it may appear." In this way we take responsibility, we empower ourselves by acknowledging our inner power/ choice rather than by placing power outside where we can never reach it.

Meditation is an inner journey that has a profound effect upon ourselves, the people we connect with, and the planet. It is a choice that requires a deep commitment. The mind has incredible energy that usually rushes from one thing to the next, so to quiet it takes perseverance. Often when we make the choice to meditate, many distractions will occur—phones ringing, people asking for our assistance—as though the universe were asking us, "Is this time important? Will you do this?"

So once we have established that we will meditate and choose a time or times to meditate it is helpful to have a special place for the practice. One can set aside a room or a portion of a room that is kept clear and free from clutter. A chair, cushion or meditation bench can be placed here. It is important to create a space of peace and to be clear in the intention to do so. Choosing each item in this space carefully and tenderly caring for it sets into motion the understanding of caretaker mind, a mind that is purposeful and loving, giving consideration that what one does in this moment affects one's own future and the future of the planet. An altar or shrine can be set up here. Place on the altar a representative of the four elements: a candle for the fire; a bowl of water to represent the sea of mind in which we all swim; incense, representing the air, the breath of life, the carrier of our prayers to the universe; salt to represent the Earth, our bountiful mother. An image from nature—a mandala, a symbol of a goddess, (Corn Mother is one that embodies the life server, who shares her bounty in service of all humanity)—may also be placed here. This helps the mind to concentrate on universal concepts of loving kindness, clarity and service. Native Americans often place a food offering of cornmeal, Buddhists place an offering of rice, in acknowledgment of the bounty we have received. This offering of food nourishes and sustains what is good for all. And each of us, from whatever tradition we are from, know in our hearts what will represent for us the honoring of this sacred energy of life.

The meditative posture is one that enhances the free flow of energy throughout the body and energy fields. Sitting in a straight backed chair with feet on the floor, sitting on a cushion with legs folded tailor-fashion or in a semi-lotus or lotus position are all postures that give one stability and keep the spine erect. Just as water flows most easily through a hose that is not twisted, so too, the life energy moves most easily through the erect spine. Many of us have weakened our bodies through inactivity and find it challenging to sit for any length of time without back support. Physical activity is important to keep the energy flowing and stretching exercises or yoga will strengthen the body. The more we practice, the stronger we become and eventually we are able to sit for long periods of time, supported by the breath rather than by furniture. It is good to sit rather than lie down during the meditations, as one is awakening channels of the subtle bodies that previously have been dormant. There is a different kind of consciousness that develops in sitting. One can note this difference by experimenting and doing the meditations while sitting and then doing the meditations lying down. If one is differently abled and cannot sit, then the meditations can be done lying down.

The nine meditations herein are offered both as a means of introducing people to meditation and as a help in deepening the practice of those who are already meditating. I suggest reading through all the meditations before commencing practice. The imagery is very rich, containing principles common to many spiritual practices. After one is familiar with the concepts, then it is time to begin the practice. To set a firm foundation it is good to practice each meditation once in the order presented. Another suggestion is to work with each meditation three times before moving to the next, working in the order presented. Once the nine meditations have been completed, work with them in whatever order feels best to you in the moment. For example, you may be working with the issue of forgiveness and want to work with "A Way of Peace" for a greater length of time. The meditations are to be worked with again and again as the insights gained become more and more subtle and more deeply affect the totality of one's being.

When working alone, read the meditation through several times to familiarize yourself with the imagery. You may want to make a tape of the meditation, using your own voice to guide you. If working without a tape, concentrate on the main concepts. For example, in "Child Wisdom" you are moving to a space of natural delight and spontaneity where you are one with all of nature. You call forth the child within yourself. So sit comfortably, relax, breathe deeply for several minutes until your mind is clear, allow the image of that child to take shape within your mind's eye, and sit with the image. It is not necessary to recall in the meditative state every word of the written meditation. As you continue your practice, and as the essence of the meditation is absorbed, the details will become clearer.

Working with a partner is another way of meditating. Have your friend slowly read the meditation to you and then exchange roles. These meditations are also excellent for working in groups. In a group situation the role of the meditation guide can be shared by the group members.

Pick a time to meditate in which you will not be disturbed. Turn off the phone, meditate in your special meditation area, and make clear to yourself that you are going on a sacred journey, a journey that is to be honored. Ask family or housemates to help you with your journey by giving you this time free from distraction. Once you have made the time, and are in the space, make a clear beginning. Some practitioners like to light incense and to bow to the energy of the universe as they begin and end their meditation. Trust yourself to find the meditation rituals that have meaning for you. Allow yourself to be guided by the inner voice and know that, as you continue your practice, insights will expand and deepen. There will also be times when your practice seems "not to work." Yet in reality it is working because you have made the commitment to sit and you are sitting. It can be likened to the practice of a musical instrument. At times the practicing of scales seems clumsy and hopeless, yet those hours of persevering practice enable the musician to play with ever greater expertise as time goes on. Using the journal pages which follow each meditation in this book to record your experience of that meditation is a good way to deepen your understanding as well as to follow your process in meditation.

During the stillness of meditation the creative energy of life flows most easily through us. In many spiritual traditions this creative energy is expressed as three in one. In the Christian tradition this is known as the Holy Trinity, the Father, the Son and the Holy Spirit. To the Hindus, it is the energy of the kundalini. In the Wiccan tradition it is the energy of the Mother, the Maiden and the Crone. Tsalagi cosmology refers to the creative energy as the three fires: will, love and active mind. The fire of will is the energy of our intention, the cause that creates what is. To strengthen the will is to make clear our intention, to know that our thoughts create cause. That is, through the energy of thought we bring into manifestation what is experienced in our lives. The will is strengthened through the remembrance of our life purpose. The second fire is love's wisdom, the energy of compassion, caretaker's mind. This is the wisdom of forgiving and giving. When love's wisdom is activated we have a heart so spacious it can contain whatever is. It is willing to forgive, to release the pain of the past, to know that we are all in process, and to stand free in the present. The third fire is the energy of creative mind. This is the power of right action—the wisdom, the intelligence, to bring into manifestation what is good for all of life. The fire of will blazes forth with the thought "I will be alive, I will make clear my intention, I recognize the creative power of my thought." The flame of love rekindled is the wisdom to see, the energy of generosity and compassion. It is the thought that says, "I honor the circle of life. I give that all may be cared for, that Earth may survive and her children may live in peace and in plenty." The fire of creative mind is the wisdom of right action: "I will create what is good for all of life."

The meditations shared in *Crystal Visions* work with the three fires. For example, in "Three Jewels of Wisdom" we make the initial exploration of the sacred fires, recognizing them as treasures within our hearts. "Crystal Visions" strengthens the fire of will, as the life purpose is recalled. The energy of love's wisdom, the second fire, is called forth in "A Way of Peace." The power of right action, the third fire, is clarified in the "Rainbow Warrior" meditation.

Each meditation is an inner journey to make a stream of clear communication between one's mind and heart. It is a creative process, designed to facilitate a deeper exploration of one's self, one's life purpose and one's connection to and responsibility for the planet. Nine meditations were chosen because nine is a balance of threes. The ninth vibration is one of universality and completion. When we are resonating to the consciousness of nine we have an understanding of the universality of all life. No longer are we responding to the energy of separation whether it be separate self or a separate nation. To live in accordance with this energy is to recognize ourselves as a planetary family and to live in harmony with the Earth and with each other.

The crystal is a manifestation of the most sacred perfection inherent within us. Many Native Americans revere the crystal as a dear friend whose energy amplifies the Creator's eye within us and enables us to feel our true vibration. The crystal has an extremely high and exact rate of vibration and can store, transmit, amplify and transform other rates of vibration. These qualities make the crystal useful in computer, communications and laser technology. Crystals are used in the simplest quartz radios and the most complex micro-computer chips. These same qualities enable the crystal to energize and heal our bodies. The electromagnetic energy of our thought is amplified by the crystal so that affirmation, visualization, concentration and meditation become stronger when working with crystals.

Many people feel called to work with crystals at this time. Crystals are great and powerful teachers for us. In the Tsalagi tradition, a practitioner works with meditation for at least two years before handling the crystals. This insures a firm foundation, a stability and strength of mind. It could be potentially harmful if the confusion, rather than the clarity of mind, were amplified.

When first meeting a crystal friend it is good to clear it of the energy of previous handlers by running it under spring water or smudging it. To smudge the crystal, burn some cedar and sage and pass the crystal through the smoke several times until it feels or looks clear. The crystal is an amplifier of our process of mind so a personal crystal that is placed on an altar or shrine is a good place to begin crystal work. Make friends with this crystal by holding it in your hands and feeling love pouring from your heart into the crystal and flowing from the crystal back into your heart. Sing or chant a sacred song to the crystal. In this way the crystal awakens and holds the memory of that sacred song and that energy of love. Then return the crystal to your altar. Each time you meditate the crystal will amplify that clarity of mind.

Crystals, formed in the center of the earth, in the heart of the Mother, were once opaque and, through a process of heat and pressure, became clear. This is analagous to our process of growth. As human beings we become clouded through our travels upon this earth. Then, through a process of heat and pressure, (the process of living) we again become clear. The light moves through the crystal in a spiral motion just as it moves through us. In this way crystals serve as a reminder of our inherent beauty and light. Through living, we learn to polish ourselves so that the inherent crystal clarity shines.

Each crystal has a specific vibration, a specific purpose, just as each human being does. The clear quartz crystal teaches us about the power of will, the light of pure intention. Working with this crystal enables us to align our will with the Cosmic Will, the energy of the universe, and to make strong our purpose that it may fully manifest for the good of all people. The vibration of the ruby and the rose quartz is that of compassion. When pain and suffering are released, the heart opens and the connection with the circle of life and caring for all in the circle is renewed. The vibration of the topaz is the vibration of manifestation, the call to right action, action that is in harmony with all life. Working with the topaz strengthens the wisdom of works that succeed.

Learning about crystals, we learn about ourselves. Most important is our intention. To come to the crystal from the place of the heart, to make ourselves ready to receive the understanding the crystal brings, we make an offering, we give up our ignorance and our attachment, that the clear light of truth may shine within ourselves and within all beings.

I have chosen the title, *Crystal Visions*, to honor the perfection within us all that we may recognize the power of our thoughts and visions to shape our destiny. The crystal vision is the vision of love that shines forth through all of life. It is my prayer that we will ever affirm our wholeness and the wholeness of all beings. May we live in love, in a world of beauty and harmony.

DIANE MARIECHILD is a mother, healer and seer. She studies the philosophy, cosmology and healing principles of the Tsalagi (Cherokee) Nation with Dhyani Ywahoo and is on the faculty of the Sunray School of Sacred Studies.

DHYANI YWAHOO, of the Ani Gadoah Clan of the Tsalagi (Cherokee) Nation, was trained from early childhood in the ancestral wisdom under the direction of her great-grandfather, grandparents and elders. She is founder and director of the Sunray Meditation Society, an international spiritual society dedicated to world peace.

LYNN E. ALDEN is a lifelong artist who received a degree in theatrical design from the University of Iowa. She is a meditation instructor and Peacekeeper with the Sunray School of Sacred Studies. Formerly from the Midwest, she now lives in Huntington, Vermont.